THE THOUGHTS OF A TRAVELLER

VEDIKA GUPTA

Dicata: vita.

Dedicated: life.

Contents

Preface

I vividly remember the day I read 'The Road Not Taken' by Robert Frost. I was in fifth grade in school, when our English teacher introduced us to the poem and by the time we finished reading it, I recall thinking to myself, "Wow. Someday, I want to be able to write poems that have meaning like this one. I want to put something out there that's not just words but has a message and has depth." Ever since, poetry, has evolved into being my safe haven. I was always sure I wouldn't be judged by what I wrote and it, at times, even helped me validate what I actually felt.

It didn't take long for my parents to notice my inclination towards poetry and they always encouraged me to share what I wrote, without the fear of being cross-questioned. That support and not just my wish to see my words and thoughts in print but also understanding that we're not alone in the world and what one might be going through, may somehow, resonate with a person somewhere else as well, prompted me to get a few of my pieces published.

I've always looked at life as a journey, each one in an entirely different setting, but still connected in a way that it ultimately shapes the individual to reach their final, and well-deserved goal. With this anthology in particular, I've touched upon different aspects and stages a person may go through as they walk through their journey and how time and certain encounters and experiences affect them and ultimately form them into their current self.

'Being alone isn't to be feared.

What is, is the vulnerability that comes with it.'

Reality

Scoffs and laughter.
That's sometimes all I hear.
Looks of judgement.
That's something that I fear.
Though I shouldn't,
I should be used to it, given the time,
But the never-ending feeling of being betrayed,
The reality of not having anyone to my aid,
It's still a sour thought for me to process,
A thing which will take time for me to accept.
"I'm better off alone anyways",
That's something I always say.

Yes, I do believe it,
But, in a place where people judge,
I'd somewhat feel better I suppose,
To have someone dear to confide in,
To have a person who can make me smile.
And a person who'll always be by my side,
But then again, reality hits hard.

Sometimes, thoughts become dreams,

And dreams become fantasies,

Just like this one's become mine.

I won't find that person,

At least not for a long time.

So, I'll be good, I know,

If not now then later.

For drowning in this misery,

Won't ever free me from its confine.

The Thoughts of a Traveller

V.Y.S.V.

Been a while since we last met,

Been a while since I last heard you,

The screen sometimes isn't enough,

Sometimes all I want is to hug you.

I know deep down its wrong,

I know deep down that you won't accept me.

Know that we're not much different,

Though I wouldn't expect much out of me.

Your writing inspired me to write,

Your book inspired me to read,

Your voice inspires me to try to sing,

And maybe even pick up my guitar again.

I miss you.

I miss your sister too.

I miss the fun in camping,

The sleepovers and the laughing,

I miss making tents and swords of paper mâché,

I miss trying to be spies and failing miserably,

You probably don't remember it.

Neither do I completely.

But those few years,

The time all four of us spent together,

Was unbeatable and utterly fun,

Never matched and probably never again done.

When we were all together,

Spending the evening trying to camp,

"V.Y.S.V.", you'd said,

As you carved it through the fresh cement.

"It'll always be there," you'd said,

But now I doubt it is.

Even if it were, it's not true now, is it?

That's what breaks my heart.

But what can I do to fix it?

Neither am I accepted,

Probably not even appreciated,

But I just hope you are.

Where ever you are, whomever you're with,

I just hope you're happy,

Happy and at peace with your life.

Conflicted

Like on a barren strip of land,

Surrounded by dullness,

She runs free in search,

She runs wild in hope.

Voices seem to be fading out,

She's unfocused and confused.

As she sees the sun fade away,

The dreaded solitude seems to creep in,

Leaving her with a singular wish,

A mighty hope for it all to come to an end.

Without confidence she walks,

In hope for someone to find her.

She's vulnerable and lost in thought,

And doesn't realise that anything could destroy her.

She's not unsatisfied with what she has,

There's no want for more,

She just feels unhappy,

And unsure of what she's worth.

Anxiety

My feet feel heavy,

My breath's uneven again.

My instincts warn me of something,

But my focus refuses to regain.

The songs playing in the background,

They seem too distant now.

With no clue what causes this,

Sometimes I try to ignore it,

Others, I try to calm myself,

But neither ever works.

The world seems to close in on me,

With no distinct way out.

Panic seizes me.

Another breath in,

I try to make it work.

Nails digging in,

I remind myself that this isn't a quirk.

Closing out everything,

I try to focus on something good;

A happy memory deep in there, somewhere,

But the first thing I grab onto isn't what I need,

The panic increases,

And I am reminded of more pain.

It leaves me with a heavy heart,

As I realise just how much is in there,

And how much I've tried to ignore.

What comes next was expected,

I can't stop it now,

I feel powerless and helpless,

With never ending tears streaming down.

But, fifteen minutes in and I'm calm.

I can hear the songs again,

My breathing is better now.

I may have prominent red and purple marks,

My palm always seems to bear them,

But they, too, will eventually fade away.

The Thoughts of a Traveller

Another breath in and I'm okay.

Its fine.

I'll be good.

And I am,

At least, I hope.

I'm aware of everything,

But I'm back in control.

I don't let it affect my day,

And mastering how to mask it,

Is something about which

I'll always be gay.

'Vulnerability increases the chances of being hurt

But with each step, there is so much to learn.'

The Villain

In the pitch of darkness,

The sound of thunder reverberates,

The drops of rain,

Feel like acid on her skin

Alone among the trees,

Which once seemed so inviting

She seems lost and distraught.

But with a will and vision in mind,

She walks ahead,

To finish the journey,

She knows will take forever to end.

She walks through it with a smile,

Regardless of what she feels.

She goes on each day,

With a goal in her head.

But she questions herself,

About how she could end up there.

And hates herself,

For not being the perfect judge.

Her perception too has wavered.

For she sees the leaves blowing

Which were once thought of as majestic and tough,

Are now objects of poison

Made to disrupt her path.

Loathing something didn't ever seem to be in her books,

Until she met him,

The villain hiding in crooks.

He found her when she was weak,

She was too distracted and in fear,

She'd already been through a storm,

And had nightmares all through the fall.

He appeared as a support,

Though hints of his darkness still peaked,

She ignored them all,

For she felt they were wrong.

With determination and might,

To overcome the storm,

She just fell deeper,

And the winter villain started to take form.

The Thoughts of a Traveller

He took place in her heart,

Giving her misery and thoughts,

He appeared to be a victim,

And she felt sorry for his fall.

His fall was old,

Too old to now affect him,

But she didn't know about it,

And continued to believe him.

That winter she was cold,

She'd frozen and couldn't thaw.

But as the summer seeped in,

She realised his intensions.

She tried to run,

But his grasp was confining.

It suffocated her,

Not letting her think straight.

While self-realisation played a part,
The only thing that helped her break free,
was mainly her pure heart.
She spoke what she felt,
She put forward her thoughts,
Acknowledging that she didn't belong,
She started looking for a helping hand,
Sturdy and strong,
One that wouldn't pull away,
But would help her climb out.

It took months for her to finally escape,
But her heart till then,
Had already been scathed.
And hearts aren't easy to adjust,
A sudden shift makes them stop.
It was frozen all through winter,
And summer didn't do much.

Regardless of what happened,
She went forward without a fault,
She was determined once again,
To find herself,
After all that had taken place.

The Thoughts of a Traveller

The path wasn't easy,

It was scary and tough,

The ground was full of insects,

The mud seemed to pull her down,

The trees had crosses and marks,

Ones that visibly weren't human.

The rivers were dark red,

The leaves were all black,

Still, she walked ahead,

With a smile on her face,

In hope to complete her journey,

And see the light shine bright again.

Reflection

What happened was months ago,
And with sheer confidence I can say,
I accept now what was done.
What has been and what is to be.

Those days are still a blur,
But flashbacks and nightmares are frequent.
I don't remember all the details,
But what I do is painful,
The only thing that is crystal clear is,
I'm not the one to blame.

I've come to terms with what happened,
Come to terms with the reality.
But words sometimes trigger me,
Specific sentences bring back sour thoughts.

The flashbacks though make things clearer.

Make it possible to put it all together.

The puzzle with missing pieces,

It finally starts to take shape.

I now see it,

I can believe he was wrong.

I vividly remember refusing,

But he was consistent and persistent,

And managed to bend my soul to his will.

Blunders?

The need for confiding in someone,

The hope that the person is not fake.

The confusion it brings upon the heart,

The sadness that follows the overthinking.

It's all a phase of life,

Something which a few can't ever get through.

Betrayal may have played a part,

And now they struggle to find something,

Anything at all to fill the void they're left with.

With a wish to not feel defeated,

And a will to feel joy again but, hurt;

It's not an easy thing to deal with.

It may seem to increase as time passes by.

And doesn't completely heal,

Even while they wait and sit by.

The emptiness that follows it,

Combined with a reality they fear,

It's enough to break them,

Make them feel unworthy and flawed

And crumbles down their world

Making them vulnerable and raw.

They may be surrounded by people who love them,

But in a cruel world like this,

At times they may feel lost.

They sometimes feel the need to hold on to people,

Especially if they were someone important once.

They may feel the need to ask for the minimum,

And usually get trapped in the other's ill-intentions.

By the time this realisation hits,

And sometimes it may take too long,

You may feel that all is lost again,

Like you're always on the wrong side of a war,

But keep in mind the tricks you saw,

The Thoughts of a Traveller

And how carefully that ambush was orchestrated.

What I can say without a doubt is,

There is always much to take away,

Even when a comet falls.

Trust

Although delicate,

The Greeks found it strong.

Widely regarded as a weed,

Dandelions are extremely precious seeds,

Which like Trust,

Don't require much to grow,

Just warmth and some shade,

And the fields would be endless.

But once it's uprooted,

You question the planter and its needs.

And only much later do you comprehend,

The lesson he was meant to teach.

We failed to realise that a lot was fake,

A fantasy we refused would ever break.

And as lovely as it seemed back then,

To give everything important to them;

As tempting as it seemed to think of them as "yours",

We failed to judge them,

And just trusted what they had told.

But now with the truth,

Having revealed itself,

You doubt that person and their apparent will,

To give up a ton to gain your faith.

In theory though, from what I believe,

No one in the world seems to be ready,

To commit to another without a bait.

Trusting someone seems to be a dream,

A wish upon a dandelion, if you will.

But the blow isn't always voluntary,

Tornados and storms too exist,

And there lies the thing about timing,

It doesn't always coincide with your plans.

Out of fear but hope to stay safe,

I now tend to believe,

Sow your dandelions indoors,

Secure it in a box if you want,

The Thoughts of a Traveller

But still be careful,

Because too much of anything, even care,

May ultimately defeat your purpose.

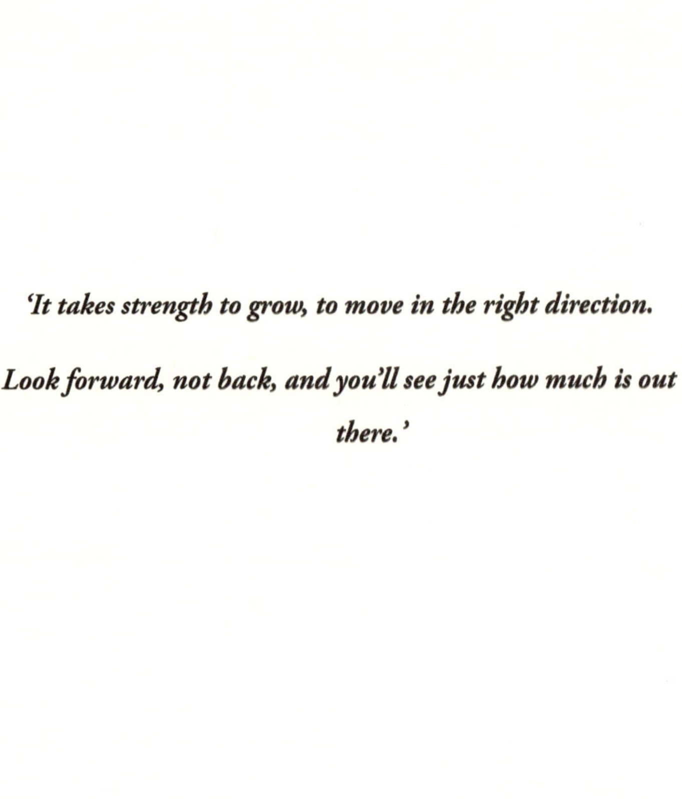

'It takes strength to grow, to move in the right direction.

Look forward, not back, and you'll see just how much is out there.'

To Two

My head's throbbing,

As the room around me seems to spin.

I could easily blame it on other factors,

A prominent one being that I was sick.

But I can't hide the truth.

If not now, it'll surface later.

I can't hide the fact,

That anxiety is what I feel at last.

Outside on a roof,

Or somewhere in a field,

Regardless of where you are,

Your effect is still pretty strong.

Time has passed by,

And more is only to follow.

For long I've stayed in thought,

But now I refuse to dwell more.

Given an option I'd take it,

If only it meant you'd not exist.

I don't miss you at all,

I just miss me before you.

I miss the person I used to be,

I miss the courage I used to have,

I miss how easily I could trust,

Without the fear of being crushed.

So now what remains is pure hate,

For my heart couldn't bear the hurt,

If not all, then a bit,

But you were aware of how I felt,

And how much I had already been through.

The spiralling seems to worsen,

When I spot the second reason.

You're not that far away,

The Thoughts of a Traveller

Just a wall and some glass in between.

Two years teach a lot,

And a few ago, I'd never have thought,

You'd get up and leave,

And never bother to think twice.

Even now when we talk,

I don't sense the guilt you say you felt.

You may have had your reasons,

But we could've stuck together.

The secret codes and language that we made,

The utterly horrible handshake that we had,

The slime we made with tide in a tiny cup,

And the photoshoots that we had.

They seemed fun at the time,

But now what's left is,

Memories of it all.

I refuse to bear the hurt any longer,

And I will for sure move forward.

Vedika Gupta

I don't have a message for you.

Except that I just hate you.

And the message I have for you is,

I'm sorry I can't open up to you.

But even what I write is barely half of me.

And it shouldn't be surprising that I feel,

You may not even be worth the rest of me.

There's one thing I'd like to thank you for,

The only thing you both taught me;

It's to be happy even when I'm all alone,

And honestly, I now feel happy.

The Thoughts of a Traveller

Emerging from the Darkness

Stuck in a maze, surrounded by darkness,

No visible light, just a deafening silence,

Often accompanied by an echoing laughter.

Nowhere to go, no definite goal,

Struggling to find the path that was once hers,

Scared to use the strong walls and vines as a guide for,

"What if they break because they don't match,

The walls of my house that are made of graphene?"

Scared and frightened she walks ahead,

Just to lose more of herself into the darkness that's spread,

Spread like a blanket of smoke or fog,

Suffocating, with no way out.

Still, she walks with confidence.

She was half-way in, when something snapped.

She was uneasy and felt awfully trapped.

There was a sudden need to grab onto something,

Something that would help her up.

And as soon as she let her pride go,

She saw the darkness turn slightly bright;
And acknowledged a star she hadn't before.

She felt joy and happiness as she saw the light,
Even if it was little, it was something right.
Walking towards it she said,
"I'm sorry for not noticing you there."
To which the star replied "I like this side a little better.
You're like a phoenix that's risen from the ashes.
You have a second chance in life; make it better,
Make it better little by little, starting with a tiny smile"

That star was like an angel,
Placed in the maze,
To make her realize,
Little things too can help make a change.
Now she walked with a different confidence,
An aura in which the only person was not her.
She took the help of the strong walls and vines,
And finally saw the light.
When she stepped out, she was not the same,
She had learned her lesson and was not ashamed.

Be perceptive and be aware,

Combined with logic,

It's a gift that's rare.

And once in control,

I can bet you'll know,

How to make differences all on your own.

Alone

In a country, a city,

A crowd or a room,

The world's a place where no matter what,

One can always feel alone.

It's a feeling.

A thought, a fear,

A nightmare.

It's unfamiliarly familiar to most.

Its dreaded but its real,

Unmeasurable and doesn't appeal.

Like a lone cloud in a clear sky,

It wanders,

But there's no one by its side.

It isn't always this way though,

Like a flower in a heap of leaves,

It attracts attention due to its beauty,

It stands out due to solidarity.

Once accepted, its peaceful,

There lies something special in the dark,

There something enticing about the unknown

And thrilling about discovering it alone.

Solidarity isn't always depressing.

There lies strength in surviving alone.

A pack is always intimidating,

But a lone wolf isn't inviting either.

With the right mindset to face the world,

Conquering it wouldn't seem impossible.

Its rather a challenge with a series of tests,

To see what exactly you're made of,

And how much you can take on.

——◆◇◆——

   The Thoughts of a Traveller

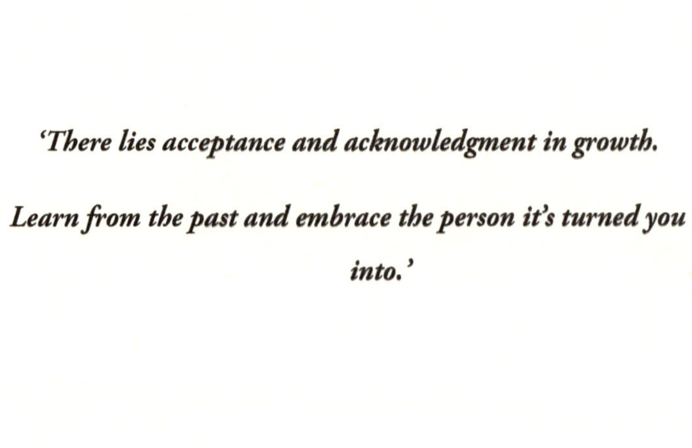

'There lies acceptance and acknowledgment in growth.

Learn from the past and embrace the person it's turned you

into.'

Peace

Isolate, but not alone.

Not always included but never an outcast.

Finally, there's some peace.

There's some joy and acknowledgment.

There lies acceptance in this process.

Not of others but yourself.

Once accomplished, you'll realise,

The never-ending storm's finally come to rest.

The turmoil within comes to peace.

And though it can't all be like a field of carnations,

Feel happy of your progression.

Introspect

Like in a field of roses,

The scent filling up your lungs,

Hair flowing in the breeze,

The sense of freedom that you feel.

The over flooding happiness,

Not being held back in the darkness,

Unaffected by the past,

Just letting go and finally embracing yourself,

It feels wonderful at last.

The grass tickles you,

As you run through the field,

The breeze soothes you,

As it carries your laughter.

It sounds different, indeed,

But it's not for anyone else to please.

Past mistakes don't affect you,

You rarely think about them any more.

The future excites you,

As you can't wait to see what it holds.

A never wavering smile spreads across your face,

One which is genuine and not so seldom now.

The glow on your countenance,

The blush on your cheeks,

The bliss in your eyes,

The intoxicating joy that you feel,

When you realise that you didn't lose,

You're regaining your confidence,

And it's visible to all that despite everything,

You're growing into someone new,

But that's a person you've learned to love.

Once you've evolved,

And learned from your mistakes,

You come out stronger than before.

You've seen the bad and have dealt with it.

The Thoughts of a Traveller

You've seen the worst and have come out of it.

You've become someone else,

And you're proud of it.

In all,

You've become You.

<hr>

Acknowledgments

And suddenly, it comes to an end…until it doesn't.

I'd say, compiling these poems wasn't the easiest task I've ever done. There were a ton of doubts and a boatload of apprehensions but, in the end, we did it.

I say we, because this wasn't an individual work. I had my biggest supporters, mom and dad, throughout, keeping me motivated and encouraged, my brother, who, is though some 7,400 miles away (yes, I did look that up), still manages to be there for me whenever I need him, and then, of course, Thor, my beloved shih-tzu, who was by my side throughout the process, while I compiled and edited these poems.

I am forever grateful to my amazing editor, Poorvasha, who taught me so much more about poetry, Katherine, and the entire Notion Press team for helping me out and making this happen.

I'd also like to thank almost everyone I've known throughout my 17 years for it was your stories, decisions and experiences that, in a way, inspired me to write these poems.

vita brevis est, poetica aeterna est.

life is short, poetry is eternal.

www.ingramcontent.com/pod-product-compliance
Lightning Source LLC
Chambersburg PA
CBHW031430160726
47993CB00003B/1492